Heart on Fire Heals the Soul

ELSIE VIOLET

Ark House Press
arkhousepress.com

Cataloguing in Publication Data:
Title: Heart on Fire Heals the Soul
ISBN: 978-1764443043 (pbk)
Subjects: POE023010 POETRY / Subjects & Themes / Death, Grief, Loss; POE003000 POETRY / Subjects & Themes / Religious; POE024000 POETRY / Women Authors.

Design by initiateagency.com

ACKNOWLEDGEMENTS

MY FAMILY

Firstly, I would like to acknowledge and give thanks, from the bottom of my heart to GOD, for gifting me with my children – Rhys & Isobel; for they are the physical embodiment of His love, grace, joy and strength in my life. They have also been a constant lesson of PATIENCE for me over the years!

I say that in the humblest way possible, because I have had to humble myself to my children a great deal for me to grow in God's love – *with* them and *for* them.

These children - that are 'of me', but are not mine, for we are all God's children first - have had to be patient with me too, as they've watched me fall and fail numerous times, and yet they love me still.

THAT is God's grace for us all.

We are *all* fallible. No-one is greater than the other…and coming from a generation of being told 'children are to be seen, not heard' – I have had to humble myself to my children and show weakness in front of them, to show God's strength in me - which also showcases God's strength in them!

Acknowledgements of the heart go out to: Grandma, Grandad, Rhys Hughes, Mason, Uncle Reya, Aunty Tina and Manaia – gone but never ever forgotten! The impact they all had on my heart was great, and the memories will be forever.

MY FRIENDS

My girls and my church family!! Where would I be without you all?!

Although you are scattered across NZ and Australia, you each hold a piece of my heart, and I am truly blessed to have been gifted and entrusted with your hearts too.

You all know who you are – thank you, and I love you.

FOREWORD

Heart on Fire Heals the Soul is a tapestry of God's truth, woven through many voices to highlight the fact that God's promises are not just for me, or about me...God's word, truth and promises are *for* all of us, *about* all of us, and *through* all of us!!

We are not alone!

This poetic collaboration of works brings together different perspectives and truths of the heart in a gentle yet fearless manner; for you to digest and reflect upon either on your own or with others.

I pray that as you read through the contents of these pages, you feel a little less alone and a little more hopeful in whatever you are travelling through this very moment in time.

My heartfelt thanks go out to my fellow co-creators – this book wouldn't be possible without you. Thank you for being willing to be part of this journey with me.

Contributors in order of appearance:

- Leanne Matton
- Emma Herring
- Hannah Mitchell
- Susan Holt
- Andrew Meek
- Isobel Joyner

Contents

PART ONE

PERSONAL PERSPECTIVES

As I lay here, words unspoken … feeling broken…
I seek God's light in the darkness – I seek His truth softly spoken.

Lord, you did not promise us life without pain,
You promised us your peace that would forever reign.

Lord, may your light in the dark keep my mind afloat…
May your truth soak my soul and keep me whole as your words replace what my mind wrote.

When all else falls and fails around me Lord…
May your armour shield me…
May your promises uplift me…
And may your love fight for me in all the places my eyes can't see, and my arms can't reach!

AMEN

OUT OF BODY EXPERIENCE – PART I
Space of unsafe

In the space of 'unsafe' where tears stain our face and fear defaces God's grace in us so much that we embrace the foetal position in that dark place our minds take us to.

Where the mind scatters, the heart shatters and the body is left in tatters on the bathroom floor…right here, in this space of 'unsafe' … our mental health matters!

COME BACK!!!
The flashbacks and negative-loop playbacks are not real!

The back-to-back cardiac attack coupled with lack of air may throw us off track
BUT, this devil's foothold feedback is a mere setback as he tries to side-track
us from the reality of God's power IN us and God's purpose FOR us!

COME BACK!!!
YOU ARE NOT ALONE!
Though proportions have been blown, our minds have flown, and our
bodies have been thrown to the floor…WE are not alone!

COME BACK!!!
REACH OUT!
Cling onto God's promises for dear life!

OUT OF BODY EXPERIENCE – PART II
Dialogue

She rocks,

Back and forth,

Pushing her bare flesh against the cold tiles,

Clinging to the reality around her for dear life as she drowns on dry land; her tears unabating.

"Come back" she hears faintly from a distance...

"I'm trying..." she whispers in response.

OUT OF BODY EXPERIENCE – PART III
She leaves...Or does she?

She got up off the floor...
She dried her weary tears...
She inhaled as she opened the door...
And she left that room where nobody cares.

Inhale...Exhale...Smile.
Inhale...Exhale...Personal exile.
Inhale...Exhale...A world so hostile.
Inhale...Exhale...Mentally defiled.
Inhale...Exhale...She's alive, but she knows this is not living.

Where am I?
What am I wearing?
What day is it?
Has time really passed?

It is not until days later that she realises...
She is still there,
Behind that door,
On that floor,
Drowning in her tears,
In that room where nobody cares.
Autopilot ... Disassociation ... High Functioning Depression

PROMISE: Psalms 9:9
The Lord is a shelter for the oppressed, a refuge in times of trouble.

PROMISE: Psalms 46:1
God is our refuge and strength, always ready to help in times of trouble

UNSEEN MARGINS - PART I
The Smokescreen

Where caffeine and routine are a smokescreen between the sheen of truth versus reality.
Where the imagery of serene green pastures mocks the widescreen machine
of unclean thoughts that demean us at the very core of who we are.

YES…WE!
I am here too!

We are the well-oiled machines behind the unseen and unclean margins,
Viewing life from the peripheral perimeters of existence.
Drowning in our own passive-aggressive pessimistic perspective of ourselves.

We are drowning, wanting to be saved…but too afraid to reach out.
We crave to be seen but continue to hide behind the smokescreen sheen pretending
to be serene…screaming on the inside, as we remain unseen on the outside.

The unseen margins…
It's lonely here, even though we are not alone.

PROMISE: Isaiah 41:10
*Don't be afraid, for I am with you. Don't be discouraged, for I am your God.
I will strengthen you and help you. I will hold you up with my victorious right hand.*

UNSEEN MARGINS - PART II
The Lines Between

Alone together, we have remained unseen while stuck between the
blurred lines of dreams vs reality, as we gleaned and preened ourselves
against the smokescreen sheen of *expectations* vs reality.

Alone together, we demeaned the truth by hiding behind the smoke-screen sheen
of rose-tinted glasses - where denial and blame became everything in between.

Alone together, both feeling unseen as we wean ourselves from this recurring dream scene.

PROMISE: John 8:32
And you will know the truth, and the truth will set you free

UNSEEN MARGINS - PART III
Something to ponder...

Who dictates the margins in a 'marginalised community'?
As an artist, I dictate the margins of my page according to the format and flow I desire.
As an author, I dictate the typeset of how the margins in my story are presented to the world.

The margins of society though?
That's a different story!

As a twice divorced single Māori woman with a criminal record hidden in my past and two adult children to different fathers; who found faith at the rock-bottom of depression and addiction born from childhood trauma ... I am a member of many 'margins' according to whoever is viewing or judging my life at any given moment.

As a child of God though, it is His love and truth alone that sees me, saves me and stretches me every single day.

THIS is the only margin that matters, because it is right here, right now - regardless of where I've been - that I make the choice to give it all to God.

All the darkness. All the heaviness. All the judgment. All the shame. All of it...
I see it...I surrender it...and I *serve* from it.

I serve, not from the peripheral sidelines of the margins, but from inside the heartbeat of whatever 'the margins' look like or feel like for myself and for those around me.

I am not my past, but I embrace who I am because the path I have travelled has brought me here today.

I have explored the boundaries of 'the margins' in my life and overcome many obstacles along the way ... not in my strength, but through God's strength in me.

From this platform of servitude, I bring an attitude of gratitude because I know what Christ has done in my life AND what He can do in your life too...IF you *choose* to let Him in.

PROMISE: Romans 8:28

And we know that God causes everything to work together for the good of those who love God and are called according to his purpose for them.

WHAT AM I DOING?

I'm emotional eating and I know it.
I know it, yet I do it, and I hate it.

The abyss is overtaking me, and I know it.
I feel it, yet I let it, and I hate it.

Fear is leading my thoughts, and I know it.
I see it, yet I do it, and I hate it.

This vicious cycle claims the lives of many.
We know it, we see it, and we hate it…

PROMISE: 2 Timothy 1:7
For God has not given us a spirit of fear and timidity, but of power, love, and self-discipline.

LITTLE LOST SHEEP

Feeling lost at sea as I walk this earth,
Waves crashing around me since my day of birth.
When can I rest Lord, when can I sleep?
When will you take me home Lord – I'm your lost little sheep.

I walk in a daze through this maze of worldly ways,
Counting down the days until you raise me up from this earthly phase.
Though I feel lost Lord, I still sing your name with praise,
For I know I am safe, and loved with you always!

PROMISE: Matthew 11:28-29
Then Jesus said, "Come to me, all of you who are weary and carry heavy burdens, and I will give you rest. Take my yoke upon you. Let me teach you, because I am humble and gentle at heart, and you will find rest for your souls."

BROKEN HEARTED

Grief holds us hostage every day,
Crippling us with tears that we can't keep at bay.
Unable to function – unable to pray,
Unable to let go of WHY?!?! – Why couldn't he stay?

PROMISE: Psalms 34:18

The Lord is close to the broken-hearted; He rescues those whose spirits are crushed.

ALL THE BROKEN PIECES

HEART: I'm scared of being spared, left to wander with unprepared feet and an impaired mind. Despite the hope declared below my layer of fear: I'm frozen...I'm fearful...I'm fragile...and I'm stuck between fight, flight, freeze and fawn.

BODY: I ache in places that keep me awake at night, but I refuse to show how I want to break for the sake of their sanity. I will fake it 'til I make it and take the stake to my heart with a smile on my face: I'm foolish...I'm furious...I'm fatally flawed...Is this my forever?

MIND: Forget-me-not as I fall through the slipknot of rot that's got me stuck in auto-play screenshot of my forever blind spot: I'm falling....I'm flying....I'm floating....Is this my freedom?

SOUL: I'm too weak to speak as the inner critique wreaks havoc in me in all directions - there is nothing I can do except seek you Lord! May your love bring peace to all the pieces of me so that we can finally exist in harmony.

PROMISE: John 14: 27

"I am leaving you with a gift – peace of mind and heart. And the peace I give is a gift the world cannot give. So don't be troubled or afraid.

HEALING THE WRITE WAY

We can *DO* everything right and still *BE* everything wrong,
We can write all night long and still be the wrong lyrics to their song.
We can live our lives according to the beat of their drums,
We can make them happy while surviving off their breadcrumbs.

Breadcrumbs of truth, love and affection…
It's a slow suicide of the soul as our heart craves connection.
Conforming to the norm of this storm as we perform like monkeys…
It's an addiction of conviction as we convince ourselves that we're not junkies for their love.

Lord, YOU are our strength, and YOU are our song,
Through YOU, we are everything right regardless of what they say is wrong.
Lord, we joyfully dance to the beat of YOUR drum in our heart,
For our life in abundance through YOU is our new start!

PROMISE: John 10:10
The thief comes only to steal and kill and destroy.
I came that they may have life and have it abundantly.

BETRAYAL OF SELF

They may have betrayed my heart with their lack of actions…
But I betrayed my soul with my delusional abstractions.
I knew what I knew but I still fell into the distractions…
Only to find the impaction of my mind created infractions of
my heart which caused the compaction of my soul!

Twas not in the hands of another that my hope should have lay,
For it is God's love alone that outweighs the sway caused by the decay
of the world that gets in the way of all that we pray for!

PROMISE: Hebrews 13:6
So we can say with confidence, "the Lord is my helper, so I will
have no fear. What can mere people do to me?"

STANDING STRONG SOMETIMES MEANS STANDING ALONE

In the farce of doing right and being right…My soul got left behind.

In the whirlwind of doing and being for the sake of others…My heart became blind.

In the heartbreak of growing and becoming…
God's truth refined my mind, realigned my values, and designed
a path that confined my destructive ways.

In this divine repositioning of my state of mind…
I felt undermined by the unkind thoughts that outlined the fact that I'm here, all alone.

PROMISE: John 14:16
And I will ask the father, and he will give you another advocate, who will never leave you

LET'S GO

I'm real, I'm raw, and I'm ready to explore…
I've learnt, I've grown, and I'm healing at the core…
I've chased, I've changed and I'm owning the floor…
I'm bold, I'm boundaried, and I'm walking through the door…

PROMISE: Psalms 27:1
The Lord is my light and my salvation – so why should I be afraid?
The Lord is my fortress, protecting me from danger, so why should I tremble?

THE BLACK ABYSS

Weaponised gratitude had my mind so skewed that I lived off platitudes
which rendered my soul confused, bruised and infused with fear.

This blackened view threw my heart to the wolves as my mind flew over the cuckoo's nest...
The lights were on, but nobody was home as reality withdrew
from view and disassociation became my voodoo.

This black abyss was my home.
Freedom was where my mind could roam.
Safety was where I could live, and die, alone.

PROMISE: Romans 12:2
Don't copy the behaviour and customs of this world but let God transform you into a new person by changing the way you think. Then you will learn to know God's will for you, which is good and pleasing and perfect.

SURVIVAL MODE

Preparing for flight with nowhere to go,
While preparing for a fight with myself as the foe.
Stuck between the two as the world turns in slow-mo,
Then freeze drops me to my knees and I stay stuck in this limbo.
What else can I do but fawn my way through another day in this flow,
I want to leave but I can't move – I'm stuck in this repetitive to-and-fro.

Fight, Flight, Freeze and Fawn...
A flesh response born from a place of self-scorn.
Strong in heart but with a soul well-worn and torn,
Nothing else to do but mourn the dawn of a brand-new morn...
...that never comes.

PROMISE: Isaiah 40:29
He gives power to the weak and strength to the powerless.

TRUE LOVE

To be in love with the love that fits my heart like a glove…
A love that comes from He who sees ALL from up above…
This is the love I chase.
This is the love that sets me free.
This is the love for you and me.

PROMISE: 1 John 4:4
Little children, you are from God and have overcome them,
For He who is in you is greater than he who is in the world.

KEEPIN IT REAL

To truly HEAL, I had to KNEEL before God and allow Him to PEEL back the layers of myself so I could see the REAL me through He who set me free.

No longer do my feelings CONGEAL, nor do I allow the others to CONCEAL my truth or STEAL my joy.

You Lord SEAL the DEAL for my soul daily, and will continue to do so until my last MEAL. You in me and I in You Lord - nothing else is more REAL than that!

PROMISE: Mark 5:34
And He said to her, 'Daughter, your faith has made you well. Go in peace. Your suffering is over.'

PART TWO

POETIC PERSPECTIVES

My worth on this earth is not defined by you or me...
Only through He who has set me free from the stranglehold of society.

I am no longer cursed with questions of my worth...
Because putting God first has burst my heart with a thirst to overcome my worst...
My vicious cycle He has reversed!

Daily prayer is a non-negotiable for me...
For this is where I give God the sea of debris within me...
And this is where I get to see *all* the ways that He continues to set me free!

DAILY TO DO LIST:

Seek first God's kingdom and His righteousness (Matthew 6:33)
Step into each day asking for God's spirit in me to lead the way (Galatians 5:22-23)
Dress myself in God's full armour (Ephesians 6:13-17)
Have faith that I can do ALL things through God who strengthens me. (Philippians 4:13)
Trust that God works ALL things together for the good
of those who love Him. (Romans 8:28)

EMOTIONS

I can choose joy for me, But I can't choose it for you.
This is something we must choose for ourselves in all that we do.

To rejoice in the hope of the Lord...
To battle fiery darts with His mighty sword...
To feel pushed back but still step forward...
To be set free as our peace is restored!

Choose God. Choose Joy.

PERSPECTIVE:

There is a time to weep and a time to laugh... A time to mourn and a time to dance...
This is what I must remember when I'm hurting and the sadness threatens to overtake my mind.

It's ok to have different feelings at different times and it's ok to express those feelings.
It's ok to cry, and it's ok to grieve; but it's *NOT* ok to live in those feelings; for that is where the darkness lies in wait, ready to lead me away from God's light on my path.

AND, while I'm in this space of hurt, I must remember that blaming someone else for how I feel will not remove the pain! Though it may be a natural reaction to blame others, and I may see others do it all the time, that does not make it right for me. God calls us not to be right, but to be righteous in His name; this notion is often-times easier said than done.

So instead of choosing to reprimand myself for being weak or holding onto the blame of what someone else has said or done, I *MUST* have a conversation with God and seek His guidance through the messiness of my emotions. I *MUST* cast my anxieties, worries, and fears to God to allow Him to work *in* me and *through* me...for it is in this space that I will find His truth, His grace, His love, His strength and His JOY!

I can choose this for myself, but I cannot choose it for you.

PRAYER: Ecclesiastes 3:4, Psalms 30:5, Psalms 118:24

Lord, may you lead us in all that we do today, tomorrow and forevermore.
Please lead our thoughts, words and actions in ALL that we do, so that we may fulfil YOUR purpose for us during our time here on earth before you call us home to you.

Help us Lord, to seek your truth above and beyond the emotions of our flesh.
May your armour protect us and shield us from the darkness of our own minds, and may the fruit of your spirit help us to love others graciously, for your glory. Amen.

GRACE

People are: Fallible. Unreliable. Prideful.
...that is me. I am 'people'.
...that is US. We are 'people'.

May God's grace lace the space in all the places I encounter,
and all the faces I embrace in this rat-race called life.
May I be reminded of my own fallibilities,
when I am faced with the incompatibilities of others.
May my life be a living testimony of God's grace,
not only alive in my heart, but also visible in my actions.

PERSPECTIVE:
In order to love and help others, I must first be willing to help myself, by working on the 'blind spots' in my own life first, with God leading my way.

I am not perfect - ***no-one is*** – and that is the beauty and brutality of life.
We are *ALL* fallen and fallible!

God sees us though; He sees all our imperfections and yet loves us still!
That is His amazing grace!

By leaning on God's love for me, I have been able to love others better; and by standing on God's grace for me, I have been able to give grace more freely ... to others as well as to myself.

To move forward in peace, I have let go of the stronghold of fear, worry and doubt that used to plague my mind daily. God's grace is enough — in me, for me, and through me.

Thank you, Jesus.

PRAYER: Luke 6:41-42, 2 Corinthians 12:9, Ephesians 2:8
Thank you Lord for the grace you gift us so freely.
Thank you for your unwavering and unconditional love.
Even though we are fallible and fallen beings – every single one of us – you love us still!
How blessed we are, to be covered by the power of your grace!

Please help us Lord, to gift others with the love, grace, forgiveness and mercy that you give us so freely. Help us to always seek you and CHOOSE you Lord, above ALL circumstances that we may face in our every-day lives. Amen.

LOVE

In my pain and in my grief,
My words were pilfered by the thief.
The one who comes to steal, kill and destroy,
Invaded my heart and stole my joy.

With no words I could not pray,
I felt segregated and separated by things I couldn't say.
But You heard the groanings of my heart Lord,
You drew me near even though my thoughts were untoward.

I was not, and am not, ever alone,
Time and time again Lord, this is what You have shown.
The thief may try, but Lord, you always prevail,
Thank you, Jesus, for your love that will never fail.

PERSPECTIVE:
I AM NOT ALONE!!

Even when I feel like an unseen wallflower, camouflaged into the patterns of the margins in our society … I am not alone. WE are not alone.

Even when I feel like an unheard whisper, drowned out by the voices of the margins in my family … I am not alone. WE are not alone.

Even when I feel down and out, with my heart turned upside down and inside out, and my head so filled with doubt that God's voice feels drowned out… I am not alone. WE are not alone.

Thank you, Jesus.

PRAYER: Psalms 46:1, Joshua 1:9, Isaiah 41:10
Thank you Lord, for never leaving us alone!

Thank you for being our soft landing when we fall, for being our strong pillar when we get up again, and for being the wind beneath our wings when we're ready to fly again.

Thank you, Lord, for your unending patience and unwavering love; for even though we fail at many things daily, you love us still. I am so thankful for your amazing grace! Amen.

HOPE

Lord... You can... You do... You will!!

Amidst the uphill battles and the downhill spirals...
Your grace dwells in the foothills of my mind.

Amidst the fear that spills into my heart and tries to kill what I am
yet to fulfil through You... Your peace stills my mind.

Amidst all these things and more Lord...
Your strength fills my soul and renews my mind, every single time.

Thank you, Jesus!

PERSPECTIVE:

HOPE in the face of adversity... HOPE in the face of fear... HOPE in the face of trauma recovery... **HOPE** ... Such a small word that can have a HUGE impact in our lives ... if we let it.

No longer am I imprisoned by my own mind.
No longer am I a slave to my past or the past of those around me.
No longer am I afraid of what the futures holds.
No longer am I under the thumb of who 'they' say I am.

Why? ...Because the proof is in the pudding of what God has already done in my life, which has set the tone of HOPE for each step forward I take; no matter what I'm facing at any given time.

My identity lays not in the labels that the world or society gives me, for I know that amidst all my imperfections, God made me in His perfect image! I am not who 'they' say I am. I am a child of God. I am a woman of God. I am me. I am free.

HOPE ... such a small word that had a HUGE impact in my life ... and still does to this very day!

PRAYER: Jeremiah 29:11, Romans 15:13, Psalms 39:7

Lord, I was imprisoned in my own mind for so long, with no hope of better days ahead.
I felt so alone Lord, but not anymore!
In your love – I shine. In your strength – I stride. In your light – I see the hope for others who are struggling in their darkness.
Thank you, Lord, for freeing me from MYSELF!
Thank you, Lord, for being the light in my darkness and for teaching me who I am in You. Amen.

THE POWER OF PRAYER

Stomach churning... Gut instincts burning...
This is not what I was yearning.

The noose removed... The aching soothed...
Lies unglued as God's truth ensued.

To breathe again... To feel strength within...
Life restored in one tiny word: AMEN
Thank you Jesus.

PERSPECTIVE:

Prayer can change your life! I can say this with confidence, because it changed mine!
Prayer can take that gut churning and twisting feeling from your belly, and the strangled feeling of an invisible noose from around your neck, and replace them with HOPE of better things to come!

How? By realising that prayer is not a checklist of requests, but a conversation with God!
Much like how you would confide in your Mum or your best friend, your prayers are a safe place to be raw, vulnerable and truthful with no filter; knowing that with your heart in God's hands, you are seen, you are worthy, and you are loved unconditionally. Through daily prayer in this safe place of vulnerability, your relationship with God grows with each next step your prayer-life leads you to.

I didn't always know this wonderful feeling though! Once upon a time, 'prayer' was just something done by others, and sometimes uttered around me. My interactions with God back then were more of an observation and a curiosity rather than a relationship.

Now though, that couldn't be farther from the truth!
God is in every single part of my life now – so much so, that I often find myself wondering: how on EARTH did God go from being a 'curiosity' to becoming my everything?!? THAT, dear friends, can only be explained as God's work – in me and around me! I can't think of any other explanation – can you?

PRAYER: Matthew 21-22, Romans 8:26, 1Thessalonians 5:17

Thank you, Lord, for showing me and teaching me what love is through my relationship and prayer-life with you. Thank you, Lord, for being my soft landing in this harsh world, repeatedly; and thank you Lord, for loving me even through my unlovable moments.
I love, because you first loved me. Thank you, Jesus. Amen.

IRON SHARPENS IRON

To see God's love through the lens of friends who upends our downward spirals and defends our soul with prayer...
John 15:12 *"This is my commandment: Love each other in the same way I have loved you."*

To feel God's love for us through them doesn't depend on trends or blends because His grace mends, distends and transcends beyond anything we could ever comprehend...
1 John 4:19 *"We love each other because he loved us first."*

To know God's love for us through them attends and mends but never pretends, because His truth is our only line of defence...
Proverbs 27:17 *"As iron sharpens iron, so a friend sharpens a friend."*

PERSPECTIVE:

To see ourselves through the lens of friends can help us in those moments where we don't feel good about ourselves - unworthy, unlovable, or unnecessary. Our friends remind us that we are loved - their hug is God's warm embrace...and vice-versa when we are there for our friends too.

As brothers and sisters in the body of Christ we pray with each other, pray for each other, and share God's truth with each other ... always on the foundation of God's love for us all.

What JOY it is, for me to call my friends 'Sisters in Christ' and truly know the depth of God's tangible love in them for me AND God's love in me for them too.

I am/we are, truly blessed! Thank you, Jesus.

PRAYER: John 15:13, Proverbs 27:9, Romans 12:10

Thank you, Lord, for the people you have placed on my path AND for the people you have removed from my path ... for both are a source of your provision and protection over my life.

Thank you, Lord, for the tangible touch of your love in my life through my friendships. I know I don't deserve everything that I have, yet you have provided love in my life with abundance, and for this, I am eternally grateful.

Lord, I pray that my life leads others to your light, and I pray that my weaknesses show the truth and proof of who YOU are first and foremost. May those around me find your light in their hearts amidst the darkness of where their minds may live right now. Amen.

REAP WHAT GOD SOWS

With my heart on my sleeve, I cleave to God's word and choose to believe His truth as a reprieve from the weave of grief that is in me and around me...

As I start to succumb to the rule of thumb that keeps me numb, I steep myself in God's word...
Knee-deep in His love I stand firm as His truth clears the fog that has my vision blurred...
Steeping in God's word relieves my weeping as I get to reap what He's sowing in my heart...
No longer numb because His love fought on my behalf and won this battle before it got to start!

<u>PERSPECTIVE:</u>
The problem is not the problem...
It is where I seek the solution from that sets the stage of next steps for me.
Staying stuck, stagnant or silenced is not where God calls me to be,
For it is in His truth alone that I am set free.

He empties me and empowers me at the same time.
He grounds me and uplifts me at the same time.
He humbles me and encourages me at the same time.
He stills me and strengthens me at the same time.

Fight, Flight, Freeze and Fawn be gone, because survival mode is not needed when I'm thriving through God's power in me! Thank you, Jesus!

<u>PRAYER: 1Chronicles 16:11, Psalm 28:7, Psalm 29:11</u>
Lord, please carry us through the darkness when we lose sight of your light.
Steep our hearts in your word and the truth of who you are to us and through us.
Soothe our souls with the songs of your purpose and promises over our lives.
Free our minds with the peace of who you are amidst the broken pieces of who we are.

Our healing journey is a lifelong adventure with you Lord, and though we will never know everything, we do know YOU, and that is enough.

Help us, Lord! Breathe your life into our lungs when it feels like the world is strangling the breath out of us! Protect our minds Lord and guard-rail our hearts.
Be our light in the darkness of the world around us and help us to be a light for others through you.

We thank you Lord, for all that you are, and all that we are through you. Amen.

GOD'S TRUTH...

It grounds me and grows me - Simultaneously.
It fractures me & frees me - Ceremoniously.
It honours me & humbles me - Shamelessly.

To expose the lies, we must first seek the truth.
Not my truth. Not your truth. Not their truth.
But God's truth!

PERSPECTIVE:

There is so much more happening in us and around us than meets the eye.
By not only seeking God's truth, but resting in it, standing on it, and speaking it out.....it takes our human focus off the lies, and exposes them by proxy!

In spiritual warfare, we need not fight against the lies, for by living out God's truth in us - He will fight for us!

We are surrounded by wolves in sheep's clothing!
Not all people that quote scripture, have Christ in their lives.
Not all people that attend church, have submitted their lives to God.
Not all people that call themselves believers, actually believe!

In God's strength alone, can we strive to survive the naivety of our minds in this spiritual warfare.

PRAYER: Matthew 7:15, 1Peter 5:8, Ephesians 6:11

Dear God, please guard our hearts and minds against the wolves in sheep's clothing around us who come to steal, kill and destroy. Please clothe us daily in your full armour Lord, so that we may be protected from all the things we can't see. Arm us with your wisdom, discernment and truth Lord, so we may be equipped to stand and fight in your name, for your glory.

Help us Lord, to keep our eyes fixed on you when temptations and distractions attempt to lead us away from your purpose over our lives. May you be the lamp at our feet and the light on our path Lord, to guide our steps and protect us from harm. Amen.

LORD LEAD MY WAY

Whatever your plan is for me Lord, let it be.
It is what it is and whatever will be, will be.
Trusting in your plan Lord, sets my soul free.

As I enjoy the moments of today,
I think not of tomorrow's guarantee.
For my heart is in your hands Lord,
Your truth is my only decree.

Where you lead me Lord, I shall follow.

PERSPECTIVE:

Control is an illusion.

The biggest paradox of my life is that to take control, I had to let go of control all together; and surrender it all to Christ!

Surrender my thoughts, surrender my feelings, surrender my opinions, surrender my conversations, surrender the situations and circumstances, and most of all, surrender the outcomes... ESPECIALLY when the fires around me and in me became all-consuming and overwhelming.

Those fires were refining me.

Those seasons were cutting off branches in my life that were not producing fruit.

By letting go of my desires, I have set a fire in my heart that will set my soul free.

PRAYER: Mark 9:49, John 15:2, Proverbs 3:6

Thank you, Lord, for leading me through the fire as I fought the desire to disengage from the crossfire of this wildfire world around me.

As I aspire to acquire the cease-fire amidst my fleshly spitfire, may your truth be the justifier of my heart, the purifier of my soul, and the amplifier in my mind.

Lord may my words through you help me to inspire hearts as I rewire my life according to your higher way of living. Amen

LIFE AND DEATH

Inhale, Exhale – my breathing laboured,
Inhale, Exhale – the darkness favoured.
Inhale, Exhale – the numbness savoured,
Inhale, Exhale – my sanity wavered.

Inhale, Exhale – my reality unforgiving,
Inhale, Exhale – I'm alive but not living.

PERSPECTIVE

Inhale, Exhale... Autopilot.
Inhale, Exhale...Lost moments of time.
Inhale, Exhale...The rhythm of my disassociation.

Each breath is merely a survival mechanism as my mind creates a wall between consciousness and reality. Where the numbness I feel is both a refuge and a prison because even though it disconnects me from my grief, it also disconnects me from the world and the ones I love that are in it.

To be present in the moment and STAY present, is a struggle as I juggle my emotions that I want to run away from, while running towards the explosive emotions of others who are drowning in their grief too.

Lord, give us strength!
Breathe your life into our lungs.
Replace our numbness with your love.
Bring us back to life through your spirit in us Lord.

PRAYER: John 6:63, Proverbs 8.35, Psalms 150:6

Lord, be my anchor when my mind starts to float away.
Anchor me in your truth and promises Lord, so I can shine your light into the darkness that we're all feeling through this grief.
Breathe your life into my lungs Lord, so I can breathe your promises into our home and into the hearts of my children who need your strength just as much as I do. Amen

PART THREE

PEER PERSPECTIVES

God speaks to us ***all*** in so many ways,
His voice brings light to our darkest days.
Broken roads become purposed delays,
And rock bottoms become our place for praise.

God is so much more than just words in a book – God is His word planted in our hearts! He is with us in relationship, connection, ongoing conversations, and in our stories shared that become testimonies of hope for those around us … and even though we are all different as human beings, God is the same for us all! Isn't that amazing?!?

How does God speak to you?
How do you feel anchored, led, guided, guarded, protected and provided for through Him?

Journey with us over the next few pages of PEER PERSPECTIVES, where stories are shared about how God has moved in the lives of others! It is such a privilege to be able to witness how God's light shines in those around us.

NAME: Leanne
AGE BRACKET: 50-60
OCCUPATION: Psychologist

I have known God as the creator of the heavens and earth and of humankind since I was 18. Looking back, I see that he had been revealing himself to me for some time, and in my brokenness, I came to him in surrender. In response, he made a way where there was none and I found more than a temporary comfort, because he invites us to come into relationship with him through the gift of the Holy Spirit.

Rather than having an intellectual understanding of who God is, I came into an embodied relationship with him, just as his early disciples did. With his spirit dwelling inside me, I had a revelation of the nature of God through understanding his salvation plan, and an assurance of a sovereign power who paid my debt in full. Even in a fallen world, as we live separated from his kingdom, I have the comfort and hope of knowing he will bring about a new heaven and a new earth, and that the life he intended for us is still ours.

Even decades later, he continues to go before me, lifting me up and covering me, providing refuge and shelter under his wings. Although there is tension between the world and God's ways, he reminds me that he has overcome the world, and I am never alone. No longer separated from these eternal promises, I move through life according to his ways, not my own, knowing I don't have to earn anything. Through his grace and the immense sacrifice of his only son, who took our place to save us from the power of sin and the sting of death, we walk in victory and the assurance of eternal life.

Having a personal relationship with God not only heals, guides and comforts, but it means I have an answer for those still searching, able to offer a place to find peace, joy and hope through his word. Even nonbelievers call to him in times of need, and he answers. When his creation cries out for him, he reveals himself to us as an eternal living spirit. If we continue to seek him, we are given all the gifts of the spirit, including a private prayer language for those things that can't be expressed in words.

Once reconciled, nothing can separate us from his love because he is the same yesterday, today, and forever. Even as we live subject to death and decay, and as anarchy reigns around us in this post-Eden world, it is well with my soul.

NAME: Emma
AGE BRACKET: 20-30
OCCUPATION: Environmental Consultant

Sometimes I feel like I am living in two worlds.

When I look out into a park, some days I see purple flowers that represent invasion. Green vines that seem to suffocate everything around them. Dark, ominous clouds that bring destruction. I see cigarette butts and food packaging scattered carelessly around. Ballons that will one day catch in the throat of an unsuspecting turtle. Dishevelled ibis, barely surviving in their post-apocalyptic existence. Pain and suffering infiltrate every corner of the world. And that is just what I see in front of me. In the back of my mind, I see flashes of articles. Genocide. Violence. Degradation. Injustice. How can anyone survive this world? I am simultaneously driven by anxiety and frozen by depression. How can I do anything but drown?
My truth is that I can't. Not on my own.

Other days, days that are gifted to me, that park is transformed. I can see the beauty in both the native host and the foreign strangler vine. Clouds bring much needed respite from the heat, and rain for growth. Winds test us to make us stronger and give us space to breathe. I can see litter and not assume the worst of people. I can acknowledge the joy that a bouncing balloon brings to a child on their birthday. I see the resilience in God's creation, in the ibis adapting to thrive despite so many obstacles. I see God's love materialising in the most unlikely places, through selfless generosity and sacrifice. I don't see an absence of pain. I see resilience. I see hope.

There was a time in my life when I thought that being a Christian meant no longer feeling the pain and suffering of this world. I thought, and I prayed, that God would give me a life full of joy if I followed him. But that isn't quite what he promises us. He gives us hope in the midst of suffering. He gives us joy in the midst of pain.

And so, I hold on. I hold on to the knowledge that I will one day get to see the creator's creation in its full glory. I hold on to the knowledge that one day I will get to see a world without decay, without violence. In perfect harmony and justice and peace. I hold on to His love. I hold on to His joy. I hold on to His plan.

I still get distracted by the hurting in this world. It still breaks my heart. But instead of drowning in it, God is showing me how to swim. He gives my weary heart rest; through the loving community He has placed around me. He gives my despairing heart hope; by showing me glimpses of His plan and how He is working through us to restore His creation. He gives my panicked heart grace; by acknowledging my own brokenness, loving me regardless, and filling the gaps Himself.

He gives life, where otherwise there is death.

NAME: Hannah
AGE BRACKET: 20-30
OCCUPATION: Pastor

My testimony has its ups and downs like anyone's, and through it all, I KNOW that God has always been present in my life.

I was born into a Christian family and have been involved in church since my infancy. I have always known that God loves me and sent His son Jesus to die for me so I could live forever in God's family. I have known for pretty much my entire life that God is my creator, my heavenly Father and the all-powerful being holding the universe in His hands. But for a long time, I only understood these things intellectually. It took a while for my heart to catch up.

I must have been a budding teenager when I cried out to God asking Him why I wasn't 'on fire for Jesus' like my peers were. I didn't 'feel God' or anything like others described and I desperately wanted to. I didn't have any tangible spiritual experiences yet that I could refer to that would help me see that God was at work in my life. I felt very much that God was silent.

Fast forward to my early years of university, where I don't exactly know what happened, but in reading the Bible more, and spending more time alongside like-minded Christians, and sharing the good news of Jesus with others - I felt the fire within that I longed for. God revealed Himself more and more to me, and I searched more and more for Him, to understand and know more of Him. Since then, God, in His kindness, continues to show me in small ways and big ways who He is. He has provided, protected and guided me even when I couldn't see it.

Time and time again, God has placed the right people and circumstances on my path, so that I could see His goodness and His love for me and open my heart to Him. He has led me to a church family who loves, supports me and encourages me to grow in my faith, and I also have the privilege to encourage others in their faith as we do life together. God has placed me within this church family to both be encouraged and to encourage others.

I have the joy of leading a ministry, where each week the team and I bump shoulders with people who may not know Jesus yet. We have the great opportunity to show God's love in word and deed. Through this ministry, God has led me to many deep conversations with people - some, where I can simply be a listening ear and show them that I love and care for them, and others of a spiritual nature where I can invite people to consider investigating Jesus for themselves.

I am by no means a finished project. I am learning everyday more of God's character, His love for me and how to live the good life as He intended. And as I learn, I am surer than ever that I am a dearly loved child of God. I am certainly much more aware of the weight and ramifications of that now than when I was a child/teenager. Now, I have a much less hard time trusting God in my everyday life, because He has proven His trustworthiness through His word, and through my life up until now.

NAME: Susan
AGE BRACKET: 50-60
OCCUPATION: Radio Show Host

I grew up in a semi-rural area north of Brisbane. While my upbringing wasn't particularly Christian, my parents took my sister and me to Sunday School when we were young. I also joined Girls' Brigade, and it was through that community that my early faith began to take shape. I kept going to church after I left the group—not because of a deep conviction at the time, but because I wanted to stay connected to the friendships I'd formed.

But something deeper began to stir. As I learned more about God, I found myself drawn into a relationship with Him—one that has become the foundation of my life. Looking back, I can see how faith softened me, grounded me, and ultimately transformed me.

At first, I thought I stayed with faith because of friends. But over time, I've come to know God as my safe place—my anchor through both calm and storm. I've seen miracles, watched lives change, and witnessed God move in undeniable ways. But the most powerful work He's done has been within me: drawing me out of fear and into freedom.

For years, I lived for appearances. I cared more about how I was perceived than who I actually was. Fear of rejection and judgment shaped my decisions. If you've ever lived like that—constantly adjusting yourself to gain approval—you know how exhausting it is. It leaves you vulnerable to compromise and disconnected from your true self. In fact, I'd say it left me not really knowing myself! God's truth has reshaped my thinking and my life, and two principles have become central to that journey: fearless responsibility and wholehearted authenticity.

Fearless responsibility means owning my choices, without shame or blame. It doesn't mean I get everything right, but I live with confidence that, even when I mess up, I'm loved by a God who is steady and safe.

Authenticity, to me, means living in alignment—between what I believe, what I say, and how I live. That alignment grows stronger as I continue to read and respond to God's Word. When your life is rooted in truth, you no longer need to chase approval.

It's freeing to release control of your reputation. Even Jesus—surrendered, served, sacrificed, and suffered—was misunderstood and rejected. But He stayed true, and His life continues to change the world. That's the model I aim to follow.

Today, God entrusts me with platforms as a coach, author, speaker, worship leader, and mum. He has given me stories—of beauty, brokenness, and freedom—to share. My deepest joy is to pass that freedom on, helping others live fully, fearlessly, and free.

PART FOUR

BEHIND THE MASK, BELOW THE SCARS
PRIVILEGED PERSPECTIVE

My heart on fire for the Lord has healed my soul and kept me whole despite the holes in the world around me.

As the world around me took its toll on my soul and stole precious moments of my life, these pages bore witness to how God's love created a keyhole of light in the hellhole I used to think my life was at the time.

Little did I know that the little keyhole of light would ignite the coal in my soul into a flame that would fuel a fire, not only in *my* heart, but also the hearts of those around me.

My heart on fire for the Lord has healed my soul and put my suspicious eyes to rest, as I realise and embrace the fact that my faith journey is not about me – it is about *GOD THROUGH ME*!

Thank you, Jesus, for all that you are and all that I am through you.

This chapter in Suspicious Eyes Taints the Heart took you to the dark parts of my past, to help you see me, know me, and understand the parts of me that I had only just started to unpack and understand myself. This time, it will be same-same, but different.

This time, I want to highlight the LIGHT that was also in my life back then, even though I didn't see it at the time because I felt so overwhelmed, overtaken, and overshadowed by the darkness around me.

Hindsight is such a beautiful thing when looking back with the lens of God's love though, because despite the darkness that surrounded me as a child, I can now clearly see the little rays of light and the soft whispers of hope that were planted in my heart for a life outside the suffocation of dark clouds that followed me everywhere.

- I had Uncle Raymond, who showed me what goals were just by having a job.
- I had Aunty Tina, who showed me what love in action looked like by consistently driving from Whangarei to Auckland and back just so I could spend the holidays with her.
- I had Grandma, who showed me what friendship looked like by including me in her regular trips to her friend's house across the road for dinner (where I got my first taste for spicy food!); and by sitting with me in the kitchen playing cards and drinking unsweetened lemon juice from the lemon tree in her backyard.
- I had my friend's parents, who showed me life in God's light by welcoming me into their homes when I left home as a teen with nowhere to go; who showed me kindness even though I had nothing to offer in return.

None of these people could see the value of their actions at the time - they were just being who they were - and every day, I thank the Lord for their seeds of love and grace sown when I was younger, because it all helped to shape who I am and where I am today.

Based on my upbringing and my surroundings, I could have easily gone down the path of addiction, gang relationships, and early death by suicide.... but I didn't. Often-times, I find myself wondering how I'm still alive today after all the destructive decisions I made along the way; and I truly believe that these people had a part in saving my life without knowing it.

Now, in my 40's, I have the privileged perspective of being a light for those around me in almost all the same ways that I was blessed with back then!! The irony is not lost on me with how my life has come full circle. I may not see the fruit of my actions in my lifetime, but I sure do see the value!

> **Romans 8:28 NLT**
> "And we know that God causes everything to work together for the good
> of those who love God and are called according to his purpose for them."

PART FIVE

PRAISE PERSPECTIVES

Some days I wake up and I know nothing...absolutely nothing!
My mind is empty, my heart is heavy, and my soul is uneasy...
I *know* nothing, but I *feel* something, and I have no idea what to do...
I know there is nothing I *CAN* do, except seek God's grace in this space as I slow my pace and place my heart in His hands, so I can face whatever this is in His strength.

Lord, may you replace any trace of disgrace with laces of your grace
in all the spaces that debase your truth in me and for me.
Help me Lord, to embrace your love in the face of the black
abyss that threatens the crawlspace of my mind.

Psalms 90:14-15 NLT
"Satisfy us each morning with your unfailing love, so we may sing for joy to the end of our lives. Give us gladness in proportion to our former misery! Replace the evil years with good."

TESTIMONY THROUGH POETRY

Writing sorts my thoughts and aborts the mission of my flesh reactions
as I put my heart in His hands through poetry.

Writing heals the hurt that conceals my heart
and kneels the ego of my flesh before Him through poetry.

Writing releases the pieces of pain that cloud the peace in my heart
and increases His strength in me through poetry.

Thank you Jesus for this gift of writing that glorifies YOU in me....
Who I was, who I am, and who I am yet to be...
A living testimony through poetry.

THE SHIFT

Using my voice became a choice and a chance to rejoice,
For speaking God's truth without reproof broke the silence
that enabled the violence IN me and around me.

By seeking God, I found myself,
And in His strength, I began speaking up without sneaking out on myself!
No longer do I live in the shadows of meek or weak,
And no longer do I continuously seek the good in my life,
For I can SEE it, and I can FEEL it now, every single day.

Thank you, Lord, for being the strength in my voice & the reason to rejoice daily.
Thank you, Lord, for the gentle way you speak to my heart & tweak my mind daily.
Thank you, Lord, for the tangible proof of your truth in
my life & all the ways you love me daily.

THANK YOU

In the hardness and harshness of the world around me,
I thank you Lord, for your softness that grounds me.
In the sorrows and sadness of the world within me,
I thank you Lord, for your peace that uplifts me.
In the fear and fretting of what lays ahead of me,
I thank you Lord, for your courage *in* me and your encouragement *for* me.

You never promised that life with you would be easy Lord,
But you did promise that you would never leave nor forsake me.
And though I've still met challenges on this faith and healing journey,
I have never had to walk alone in the dark without hope like the old me.

IF ONLY WE KNEW

If only we knew…
That we could defuse hostility with the mobility of humility through the stability
of God's strength *in* us, and the tranquillity of His peace *through* us.

If only we knew…
That we stumble off God's path when we fumble His truth and jumble it with pride while we
grumble about others, instead of being humble before He who first humbled Himself for us.

If only we knew…
That regardless of the tears cried in our heart or dried on our face, God's
truth is denied when pride is the guide that causes divide.

But hang on a minute…We DO know this!!
And yet we *still* fumble, we *still* fall, and we *still* fail!

THANK YOU, LORD,
For your unwavering love despite the lies we hide inside that collides with your truth.

THANK YOU, LORD,
For your love that abides in us and guides us even though our pride renders our hearts uncouth.

WHERE GOD GUIDES, HE PROVIDES

As God guides and provides, I find myself tongue-tied and wide-eyed in absolute awe of where I am, where I've been where He is leading me next.

What an adventure life is with God's truth applied to my every stride as I decide to confide and abide in Him daily.

Thank you, Lord, for the tears I cried as the old me died while you closed the divide between my pride and the shame in which I no longer hide.

Thank you, Lord, for all the ways you continue to guide and provide in my life.

JOY IS NOT A GIFT TO BE RECEIVED – IT IS A GIFT TO BE LIVED!

Thank you, Lord, for waking me up today.
Another day = another opportunity to step into the purpose you have ordained for my life!

——

Lord, thank you for showing me that my relationship with you is the most important relationship in my life, because through you, I can love those around me better; and through you, I can see me and BE me freely.

——

Thank you, Lord, for loving us ALL the way you do … individually and collectively! Our faith journey is not about us, it's about loving others through you who loved us first … and I pray that through your strength in me, I will be able to honour you in the way that I love others … for your glory Lord, not mine.

——

Thank you for showing me Lord, that my faith journey is not about what you can do FOR me…it's about what you can do THROUGH me! My life is in your hands Lord.
YOUR PLAN. YOUR PURPOSE. YOUR TIMING. YOUR GLORY!

——

Lord, thank you for your light that fights the darkness of my mind every single day. Sometimes I look back at where I've been, not to dwell in the darkness, but to revel in the proof of the truth of your light that shines within me. I am truly grateful.

——

Thank you, Lord, for the doors you have closed in my life.
I know that this is part and parcel of your provision, protection and plan for me.
I trust the doors closed AND the doors that will open as I step purposefully into my growth era with you. Where you lead me Lord, I shall follow.

——

Thank you, Lord, for the freedom I get to live through your word, your truth and your promises! For though the world may be cruel and dark at times, it is the imprisonment of my own mind that keeps me trapped in the stranglehold of the darkness in the hearts of others.

——

To know your truth Lord, and not to live it, is a tragedy! For I can see now how I often stood in my own way of the peace that I was seeking…even though the answer to all the questions I had was right in front of me all along – IN YOU!

——

Thank you, Lord, for your unwavering, unconditional, and unending flow of patience, grace and mercy, as I fumbled and stumbled my way to your truth in my heart.

——

The thief comes only to steal and kill and destroy Lord, but You came so that I may have life and have it abundantly … and for that, I am forever grateful! Thank you, Jesus.

PART SIX

PRECIOUS PERSPECTIVES

MANAIA...

I struggled to breathe Lord, as I wrestled with thoughts of why I still had breath in my lungs when someone we all love so dearly did not.

For a long time, I couldn't talk to you Lord! I wasn't angry at you, nor did I blame you. I just really struggled with surrendering to your will amidst the sadness that had gripped us all.

I struggled to find joy in my days. I struggled to find things to be thankful for. And I struggled with guiding my children to you in our pain, because I couldn't explain the 'reason for good' you would have had for taking a piece of our heart away from this world when he still had so much life to live and love to give.

I couldn't speak. I couldn't pray. I couldn't engage with the world. And the rolling darkness of 'the black abyss' threatened the peripherals of my mind.

The only words I could say were 'Lord give me strength'. Strength to get out of bed. Strength to get out of the car. Strength to comfort my children without falling into a heap alongside them. Strength to eat. Strength to smile. Strength to ask for prayer. Strength to ask for help.

PSALMS 38.8 *I am exhausted and completely crushed. My groans come from an anguished heart.*

1 CHRONICLES 16:11 *Search for the Lord and for His strength; continually seek Him.*

THE STUCKNESS OF MY SADNESS

Stuck between feeling everything and nothing all at the same time.
NUMB.

The hum of the world continues while life as we knew it crumbles and
tumbles around us; the sum of all things equals nothing as I succumb
to the humdrum of what has become the new norm for us.
NUMB.

Help me Lord,
To find your strength,
To find your peace,
To find your joy.

I know this numbness is less than the life in abundance that you've promised
me Lord, but I'm not strong enough to fight this anymore.
NUMB.

Lord be my strength.
Help me heal.
Help me feel.
Help me.

PRAYER:
Lord, my heart hurts so much that I can't feel anything else in me or around me.
Life doesn't make sense anymore. I feel dumbfounded, blindsided
and numb in all the spaces where your joy used to live.
Lord be my strength.
Lord be my peace.
Lord be my joy.
Amen

PSALMS 88:9 *My eyes are blinded by my tears. Each day I beg for your help, O Lord; I lift my hands to you for mercy.*

PSALMS 18:32-33 *God arms me with strength, and he makes my way perfect. He makes me as surefooted as a deer, enabling me to stand on mountain heights.*

MOUNT GRIEF

Climbing Mount Grief one heavy laden step at a time, as sadness becomes a thief to the joy that once was mine.

The climb is steep for this lost little sheep.
The temptation of 'forever sleep' creeps as darkness seeps into
my soul and causes my heart to weep daily.

Each step becomes harder than the next, as the weight of grief
becomes a thief to the belief that joy will come again.

Lord, show me the way to your presence and peace beyond this mountain that stands before me. Guide me, Lord. Save me from this sadness that has stolen your light from my life.

PRAYER:
I've climbed mountains before Lord, but none quite like this!!
This one is HARD!!!! And I'm TIRED Lord!! I'm tired of crying while trying to pretend that I'm not, so that I can be strong for others. I don't want to be strong anymore Lord. I don't want to cry anymore Lord. I don't want me or my family to hurt anymore Lord.

Mount Grief. I never want to visit this place ever again.
Lead the way out for me Lord. Help me to lead my family out of here too please.
Be the peace and light in our home Lord.
Now and forever.
Amen

PSALMS 38:6 *"I am bent over and racked with pain. All day long I walk around filled with my grief"*

LAMENTATIONS 5:15 *Joy has left our hearts; our dancing has turned into mourning.*

I LIED...

I lied when I said 'I'm OK'...
Happy moments are now tinged with sadness, and the words 'I'm ok' feels like madness.

I say 'I'm OK' but I'm not...
Joy has become a blind spot as bloodshot eyes create a fog with which I view the world,
while grief spreads a slow rot in my soul.

'I'm OK'...
Words that are not truth today, but one day, come what may, I pray
my heart will agree when my lips say the words 'I'm OK'.

Lord, how long will this pain last?
How long will my heart stay downcast?
How long must I live my life at half-mast?
How long Lord, will it take my steadfast love in you to outshine the
darkness that has bypassed the gates of your protection for me?

PRAYER:
Lord, hear my prayer!
Draw me near in your warm embrace as I face the disgrace behind the lie.
I'm not OK Lord. Will I ever be?
Fill my cup with your joy Lord, so my smile can be proof of your truth in my life despite the lie.
I'm not OK Lord, but in your strength, I believe I can be.
Amen

PSALMS 5:1 *O Lord, hear me as I pray; pay attention to my groaning. Listen to my cry for help, my King and my God.*

ROMANS 8:26 *And the Holy Spirit helps us in our weakness.*

For example, we don't know what God wants us to pray for. But the Holy Spirit prays for us with groanings that cannot be expressed in words.

LORD GIVE ME STRENGTH

The fire in my belly has waned...
The joy in my soul has drained...
The love in my heart is stained...
The smile on my face is feigned...
Where there was once music, is now silence.

Silence masks the violence of the grief that has gripped my soul, as the subsidence of hope blocks the abidance of joy causing the misguidance of self-reliance to lead my way. I'm stuck in the rut of darkness that snuck into my heart and struck me down from the depth of my soul. *Lord, give me strength.*

PRAYER:

Lord, I'm struggling to come to you with a grateful heart because I can't see the good of taking this piece of our heart so young, while others who have lived a full life (like me!) get to breathe another day. Help me to see you amidst this pain and grief. Help me to feel gratitude in my heart again. Amen

PRAYER:

1Corinthians 16:13 NLT says: 'Be on guard. Stand firm in the faith. Be courageous. Be strong' HOW can I be strong, steadfast and immovable in my faith while dealing with these waves of grief Lord? Logically I know...but in reality – physically, mentally, emotionally, spiritually...I am feeling unstable, wobbly, on the edge...Help me, Lord! Anchor me with your love and strengthen me with your truth Lord. Take these waves and wash me clean from all the bad thoughts that are in me and pushing me off centre. Amen

PSALMS 119:105 *Your word is a lamp to guide my feet and a light for my path.*

JOHN 8:12 *Jesus spoke to the people once more and said, "I am the light of the world. If you follow me, you won't have to walk in darkness.".*

BROKEN BUTTERFLY

Broken wings do not mean broken dreams, for God's spoken word through unspoken hurt can bring light to the dark and give flight through faith to things deemed broken by the world.

The hopelessness in the brokenness creates a homelessness for my heart as the darkness takes over, but God's light pierces the night and lights my path as He leads me back home.

I'm broken…but I'm healing.
One day at a time.
One step at a time.
Thank you, Jesus.

PRAYER:

Thank you, Lord, for your strength in me that got me out of bed each day.
Thank you for answering prayer, when all I could do was ask for your strength.
Thank you, Lord, for your light on my path that led me away from the darkness
that lurked at the edges of my mind and threatened my mental health.
Once upon a time I would have spiralled and sunk into the abyss of deep
depression, but not this time Lord. Not with your strength in me.

Your provisions are not always financial Lord; I see this…I know this…and I love this.
You've provided me with your strength, your grace, your peace and your mercy
every day, so I can be there for my family who are feeling just as broken as I
am … and eventually, I know we will find your joy in our lives again.

Thank you, Jesus. Amen

PSALMS 119:116 *Lord, sustain me as you promised, that I may live! Do not let my hope be crushed.*

PSALMS 39:7 *And so, Lord, where do I put my hope? My only hope is in you.*

YOUR LIGHT = MY HOPE

I'm clawing my way back to you Lord...
With your word as my sword, I'm forging forward toward your
light, as darkness threatens the borders of my sanity.

With your word as my sword Lord...
I reclaim the reward of your love outpoured even though joy feels ignored, because your
light on my path is a record of all you have already restored in me, and gives hope to all that
is yet to be explored through the power-board of your love for me, and for my family.

Hope is my way forward...
For your light gives hope to joy being restored as I inch closer towards you Lord.
Your light is the ripcord that will slow me down while also pushing me forward.
Your light, Lord, is my only hope in this life.

PRAYER:
Lord, I seek you, and I see you, daily.
Some days, your light is too bright, and I must avert my gaze...but I still see
you Lord, and I still feel you...and I'm clinging onto you for dear life!
Your light is life Lord; not only for me, but for my family too.
Your light is hope for us all as we navigate the stranglehold of grief
that has kept us bound to a darkness that has stolen our joy.
Thank you for your light, Lord. Even on the days when it feels too
bright, because those are the days we probably need you most.
Amen.

MATTHEW 5:4 *God blesses those who mourn, for they will be comforted.*

ISAIAH 41:10 *Don't be afraid, for I am with you. Don't be discouraged, for I am your God. I will strengthen you and help you. I will hold you up with my victorious right hand.*

FOREVER IN THE NEVER

When all the noise stops,
The sound of silence becomes louder than ever...
When all the words fall short,
Everything left unsaid becomes the sieve that severs the tether of truth...
Until the retethering of His small voice draws me close,
My forever in the never becomes a reality through prose.

(A collaborative riff-off writing piece with Andrew Meek)

PRAYER:
Lord, I have a strong community of faith, but I'm struggling to engage with ANYONE right now, let alone inviting closeness with other believers... Help me Lord, to open my mind and my heart again, with the gentleness of your love, grace, peace and joy. Amen

PRAYER:
Dear God, thank you for promising to bring me peace.
In every situation, help me to continue to keep my mind on you and your good promises.
I know I don't have to be anxious about anything.
Please remind me daily of this truth.
In Jesus' name. Amen

PRAYER:
God, my heart is so heavy. I release my burdens to you.
I lay them down at your feet and surrender them to you Lord.
Thank you for holding me in my weakness and weariness.
Show me how to rest and refuel in your presence.
In Jesus' name. Amen

JEREMIAH 8:18 *My grief is beyond healing, my heart is broken*

I MISS MY BROTHER

Isobel Joyner (16)

My world went silent the day I got told,
Just thinking about all the memories that I now hold.
I ask God why He took my brother so soon,
While I sit in my thoughts that are now filled with gloom.
I wonder to myself why I am still here,
Now that death is no longer my biggest fear.
I still hope one day that Manaia will walk through those doors,
While I sit and wait alone, battling my wars.
Naia, I hope you know how much you mean to me,
You never failed to find a way to bring me glee.
You were there for me like no other,
This is not goodbye – it's 'til we meet again' my brother.
I LOVE YOU!

MY GRIEF JOURNEY *Isobel Joyner (16)*

I never knew the meaning of grief until it happened to me,
The screaming, the crying, and saying this wasn't meant to be.
They say it will never go away, it will just get easier,
But that anger I will forever hold because he just left me here.
Grief hits different for every other person,
For me it just feels like I'm endlessly hurting.
Sometimes I tell myself that this is just a lie,
But deep down I just wish I got the chance to say goodbye.
My whole world flipped that day like I never would have imagined,
And now I'm stuck here thinking 'what if it never happened?'
Everyone has their own story and their own way to cope,
And my story started because of that stupid damn rope!

PRAYER:

Lord, our wisdom is wrapped in scar tissue.
We know what we know through the pain we have travelled and the lessons we have learnt along the way; and the scars on our hearts are a forever reminder of who we've loved and who you've called 'home' to be with you. Heal our hurting hearts, Lord. Amen
Rest in love Manaia. We love you always.

www.ingramcontent.com/pod-product-compliance
Lightning Source LLC
LaVergne TN
LVHW050946080826
845145LV00004B/1427